58 POEMS

58 POEMS

STEPHEN BERG

The Sheep Meadow Press
Rhinebeck, New York

Designed and typeset by The Sheep Meadow Press

Distributed by The University Press of New England

All inquiries and permission requests should be addressed to the publisher:

The Sheep Meadow Press
PO Box 84
Rhinebeck, NY 12572

Library of Congress Cataloging-in-Publication Data

Designed and typeset by The Sheep Meadow Press

Distributed by The University Press of New England

All inquiries and permission requests should be addressed to the publisher:

The Sheep Meadow Press
PO Box 84
Rhinebeck, NY 12572

Library of Congress Cataloging-in-Publication Data
Berg, Stephen.
  [Poems. Selections]
  58 Poems / Stephen Berg.
       pages cm
  "Distributed by The University Press of New England"--T.p. verso.
  Includes bibliographical references.
  ISBN 978-1-937679-17-0
  I. Title. II. Title: Fifty-eight poems.
  PS3552.E7A615 2013
  811'.54--dc23
                              2013001107

THAT JESUS ROSE, DID NOT DECOMPOSE...AND IF NOT, IS MERELY A TEACHER LIKE TEBREST...AND ONCE MORE WE ARE OPHANED AND ALONE...IN A SORT OF HELL WHERE WE CAN DO NOTHING BUT DREAM, ROOFED IN, AS IT WERE, CUT OFF FROM HEAVEN.

—LUDWIG WITTGENSTEIN

Love never sleeps it masters me and shakes me to the bottom
    of my heart hopeless net of love
Wide-winged purple bird hurled into eternity
From the dry land built by mortal hands where once
    I'd see the flesh-gnawing fishes and the sea-snails
There's no medicine for this dead man
Who sails in a strange void
Racing through the sea
Bare-thighed graceful blind with noisy dogs at my table
The tips of spear-head touching spear-head
I sleep without a sound
She beside me
And our favorite dog
And second son
And if you stand on the cliff on the cliff
You see your heart in the boiling foam
And the shape of your life

—"Ibycus on Death," version by Stephen Berg

ACKNOWLEDGMENTS

For publishing some of these poems grateful acknowledgement is made to *Black Warrior Review, Bombay Gin, Colorado Review, The Denver Quarterly, The Kenyon Review, Poetry East, Painted Bride Quarterly,* and *Boston Review.*

"Through Glass," "Bandage," "Shoeshine," "Writing Class," "Rubber Rats," "Sticks," "Vincent," and "Homage to the Afterlife" first appeared in somewhat different versions in *New & Selected Poems.*

"Hymn" was first published in a limited edition by Tim Geiger at The Aureole Press.

CONTENTS

I

CROSSES

Everywhere I go Jesus is there
on church fronts, displayed in jewelry stores, at the end of dreary
   stone aisles,
hanging or standing, glowing stained glass or scratched on red
   brick walls, over toilets, glittering on a taxi driver's neck, on book
   covers, drawn on a dirty window.
I've doodled my own crucifix with the son of god nailed to it hund-
   reds of times, begging he'd feed my soul,
looked up to watch the clouds and seen its gold flash atop domes,
   unaccountably spray-painted on water towers, smokestacks,
across the belly of a succulent billboard tan teen clad in a bikini.
Mullions, crosshairs, cracks in pavements, wait for him.
At night, in bed, knowing the shit I am, knowing my
   flesh will be shit,
I've whispered "Lord Jesus Christ, have mercy on me"
   again and again,
imitating Salinger's *Franny,*
who, locked in a trance, on her back, repeats it silently
looking at the ceiling, believing that sole prayer will let her see God.
Every one of my neighbors is happy.
I can't help them and they can't help me.
The late night weekend parties in the building across the street drive me
   berserk with envy
while the words I vow to worship and make sing
sound like a dog gnawing, splintering its bone.

VIEWING
Remembering Jeff Marks

When I walked down the aisle to the third row
I saw the box was open, the tip of his nose
peeping over the side of the coffin,
my old friend laid out in his mahogany box.
Finally I went the last few steps to take in what he was now—toys,
Eskimo sculpture, snapshots, CDs his wife and daughters had
stuffed between the corpse and white silk, his abstract tranquil
face—were his glasses on?—hands bent in like flippers, shoes
touching, suit meticulously pressed, "him" inside it.
It was like gazing across a hushed foggy plain,
    miles of tall grass stretching to infinity,
then slow motion snow spilled off a cliff horribly me—
    abysmal, nowhere—its white pouring eerie.
I walked back and took my place in the row
on a long green velvet cushion,
Bibles nestled in racks, their black leatherette covers chipped,
some asshole popular tune piped in...
So many splendid poets—
Herbert, Larkin, Hardy, Jonson, Donne—
can pierce the reader's heart
with just the right rhyme, I thought,
my eyes lighting on hair, collars, backs, necks, shoulders,
ear shapes...

OTHERWORLDLY

How can you be here, looking like yourself,
fat, dressed in a tan tweed jacket and hat,
gabardine pants, pink shirt, whizzing past me
on a racing bike, oblivious of the rain
that blows and sways in sheets across your path?
Your face shimmers with delight. Do you see me?
You were my thirty-five-year-long heartsick Jew,
nothing now but my need to
put words where you were
over and over, in one image that's left
from blind scavenging the domain
of your not being here
so I am free to see you, flesh of the future,
and smell your wet wool
jacket and beard, drenched with rain.

THE WAY

Only way would be to lift leg as high as possible hold it
in air as long as possible until it had to come down

Only way would be like night that never fails to fall amazingly
punctual palpable darker than the day absolute guarantee

Only way would be the inner crucifix sometimes inhabited
sometimes vacant of the person nailed, identity whereabouts unknown

Only way would be to vent the scream you've harbored all
these years like a starving baby do it to your dead mother

Only way would be to see the cosmos as oneself the way a good
suit fits so comfortable you barely know you're wearing it

Only way would be to insert index finger in gently
ream until able to extract nice sized chunk

Only way would be to take one of these books strewn on this desk
and rip it page by page into a cloud of wordy confetti

Only way would be to invent new terms for breathing being here
at all so as to freshen surgically eyesight taste smell

Only way would be to pour in seed all winter long for such tiny
birds as come upon the squirrel-proof metal feeder dangling

Only way would be to sing violently how false love slays oh
unadulterated version of a life that was someone's pain

Only way would be to do Pascal's perpetual exercise of
seeking the nothing of himself pierced by the gaze of stars

Only way would be to say the only way is this erroneous
couplet-winged dumb homage to the absurd anguished hunger for

Only way would be to mouth O say can you see by the corn's early
blight What so proudly we failed and the nightlight's last

Only way would be only to laugh no more speaking never use words
again just laughter order a sandwich teach curse all with laughter

Only way would be to find that word tip of your tongue a second ago
friend's name chore child abuse crib shit appointment?

Only way would be to speak with the tongues of men and of
eagles as you drop twenties into a hat violin case paper cup

Only way would be to eat less sit more hum Om syllable to calm
the quivering mind to charm the mind into wailing *yes yes yes*

Only way would be to quit psychoanalysis substitute silent prayer each
moment like W. James' definition of a saint: "the gift of tears"

Only way would be to figure out how to become a rock star at 68
sweep the country blowing harmonica improvising wild tunes

Only way would be to eat Vincent's shadowless blazing God-harmonics
digest the primal wisdom of his wet on wet on wet plus bloody ear

Only way would be to use Dante's original wineglass as a mirror
his cleansed celestial love a ladder through dreamless sleep

Only way I'm positive the only way is the way you take & not
realize you've taken it reading the sports page stocks obits

Only way oh way of ways is to know the way is the only way you
know how it feels to wake middle of the night to a wet bed

Only way would be to change the word way to way or if not way
change it to way and say it say way way way way way

FRAGMENT OF A LETTER

Everything here is...well, progressing wonderfully.
My 5385 step therapy's up to 17.
Red roses perfect cartoon flowers in the yard.
Cataracts also ripening nicely.
Nature teaching its rabid lesson: Time.
Riding my mountain bike regularly.
Some blurts in lines that resemble poems now and then.
Celebrities untouchably beautiful everywhere in my dreams.
Last night a woman I loved seemed to follow me up an ancient stone
    road but evaporated when I looked back.
Someone else's face appeared, realer than daytime real,
and she told me, lifting her face to mine without a hint of pride, how
    beautiful she is.
Life seems to provide clues to...and I feel
obligated to detect a meaningful scheme,
as if a man should know what it means to be mankind.
A man should know. Such urgency wells up at times
not like desire but like a stranger's voice
beckoning through a grove of completely still trees
close by, easy to get to.

WRITING CLASS

The student all the way down
at the end of the long table said—
"If you were *my* father you'd
drive me crazy." "Why?" I thought
to myself, what have I done
to her to...oh, well. Then
I left the room to copy
a Lowell essay on freedom
in poetry while the students wrote
and on the way back
remembered the story
about her cop father's pink
Harley, and about how much
she loved him. But something else
kept coming to mind,
though I still can't find the words—
Isn't it strange how we can resent
or fear another's mind?
It's like hating the weather
because it's cold or glary,
or like not having money
to buy a dress you want
or a custom made suit—
Maybe why he chose pink
and how it feels to ride the thing
wide open without one thought
was the "something else." We sit
thirty feet apart. We write.
The table's cluttered with white sheets.
Head down, I hear
ballpoints rolling against wood,
even the faint roar
of her old man's hot exhaust
and its bleak equivalent
all alone all alone

BAG

One gold embroidered star crown above star embroidered
Lions on hind legs left side right jaws wide their long
    tongues flames
old pouch of manhood equipment for prayer Jews give their boys
my dad's tfilin shawls yarmulkah stuffed into blue velvet
hung on a nail above my desk—

you wind the leather thongs on your arms like veins
you drape the tasseled silk white over your shoulders
you perch the black silk cap on the back of your head—

say consciousness is what you know you know about yourself and
    what you don't know yet's a second you, doomed, reckless, free
in acts of ruinous change
in texts of unheeded babble
in the dry dirt of flower pots
in the sanctification of this now this you

in the blind voraciousness of the Jew deciphering texts forever
as if the world will never be enough without those holy
    words not really real
as if beneath his eyes that ancient tortured voice of the
    infinite unknown
could guarantee God's absolute primal presence
could seize it like a butcher grips a chicken's neck
slashes the blade across it
really real

LAW

Easy to deny it's impossible to be who you are
Though you know you're not the "you" you know you are
even memory of events you know define who you are
don't really prove it but prove who you are
is at the mercy of a force you've never seen so you are
not organized like a finch or squirrel whose lives are
determined and true in unselfconsciousness while you are
always sitting on the chair edge of your mind are
worried ceaselessly by nothing in particular are
the nameless hero of a future age whose virtues are
imageless black and white negatives of faith a being so
   strong you are
joyless cold and have no need are
suffused finally with the banal godless knowledge that you are
hopelessly unknown warped adrift gutted and are
grateful for it because at least the humiliations are
precise keys that fit real brass locks on doors behind which you are
safe the word is safe & purge you of delusions shields
fending off sorrow that you are
the one whose inmost wish is to be here as you are

SUNDAY AFTERNOON

Watching TV, reading *Twilight of the idols,*
as usual looking for a clue to what to do
or think or what kind of man to be and who
should I really read to find what I seek and use it,
at least fifteen books open on my desk,
a coffee cup, my pens, some desperate notes
not to forget CoQ10, toilet paper, wheatgrass,
then back to The Shootist, any violence will do,
then out to buy chili, milk, cheese,
egg salad, thinking nothing (Zens say do this)
wondering why it all turned out like this
instead of my deep fantasies of cash and condo,
rich piece of ass supporting me in style
while poem after poem flows out of me, screw

perfectly each time, so she worships me, then
stumble on "The Four Great Errors," section 8:
"One has deprived becoming of its innocence if being
in this or that state is traced back to will, to intentions,
to accountable facts....Men were thought of as 'free'
so they would become guilty....Christianity is a hangman's
metaphysics....*No one* is accountable for existing at all,
or for being constituted as he is, or for living
in the circumstances and surroundings in which he lives....
The fatality of his nature cannot be disentangled
from the fatality of all that which has been and will be....
In reality purpose is *lacking*....One is necessary,
one is a piece of fate, one belongs to the whole,
one *is* in the whole..." and think—*That's it!*

Everything stays the same is the truth of truths;
everything changes whether you believe it or not.
Take today with its bright saucepan sky, humidity,
September dying into itself, each leaf
hitting the ground, clouds scurrying, desire
attached to nothing possible anymore.
Take it and do what? It is, each leaf
a separate *koan* to be solved by nature.
Maybe that's the right way to think of things.
3 o'clock. No-mind. Reality a pure question.
Upstairs my tenant running the clothes dryer.
Propped up next to Whitehead's *The Function of Reason*
Dogen's *Shobogenzo* next to a snapshot of Sydney and Ivy
crawling through a yellow nylon tunnel smiling at me.

FRIDAY

I walk the streets drunk *me me*
windows stare both ways: into the souls of houses into my sick soul
not one door opens not one mouth states what its owner urgently
    needs
I walk the streets throat stricken with grief and ragweed
I reach into a pocket for bills change and get lint
even the roofs know more than I do have more feel more
even my invisible eyebrows understand why what is is
the whole universe shimmers in a cheese shop window bread rolls
    thick yellow wheels crackers
The Real fused inside that thin sheet of glass between
    on either side desire sucks and bites its image until it faints
I know some innocent young driver will turn soon hit me crossing
    on the green
or the opposite: I'll stagger into a church kneel pray convert be
    thrown down by God onto the stone floor chewing my hands
I imagine too a duplicate me thriving in a penthouse no schedule
    holding out two filthy hands begging for pennies dimes a kiss
    sitting on the threadbare pillow my mother gave me the week
    before she died the red word LOVE embroidered on a blue field
a brand-new Bible pinned under my right arm
my left hand fingering Mazzaro's Annals of Human Peace
one white straggly ostrich plume drooping from my hatband
I walk the streets drunk enter a shop accuse the optician of selling
    me black-lensed glasses for the blind
buy sardines The Nation Playboy Art in America Vitamin B 12
    remember Chimes's ethereal gray silhouette of Jarry on a bike in
    heaven his forehead branded with a stargraph
buy one pair ten dollar socks periwinkle three bananas at Sue's
    multi-grain bagel carrot juice
I walk the streets drunk adding up this and that subtracting them
    too but from what?

I even take out my cheap Revlon nail clippers stop shorten my nails
    believe my soul is clean cleaner than Augustine's the man who
    told so much of himself he became God-time
I walk the streets split like a goat's hoof
    one timeless cry to WhoeverHeIs guttering in my poor belly and
    on someone's calendar my name penciled "Monday lunch noon
    probably"
and in someone's head a pious phrase from my unpublished
    masterpiece "Awe"
I wait face down in a pillow eyes shut tight

TAILOR SHOP

Spools, needles, buttons, patches of cloth.
the electric sewing machine's bullet-like nose.
I ask the tailor if he'll reinforce a button
no not now bring the coat back later—
a thousand shirts, pants, jackets hang
from a running track that takes up nearly the entire ceiling
steam squirts from a clam-like contraption
that stinks and smooths out fabric—
I'm hypnotized by the melody
of such everyday prayer it's only recognizable
as clothing—the tailor drags on a butt—
so many non-existent people
my coat folded neat over one arm ready to be worn
like every empty item on the track.

NOTES AT EVENING

Burn it crumple it trouble with words
they don't say how to live I sing I cry
of me and him of her and you
of we us them and they
nobody fathoming who is who
press pencils ballpoints felt tips
hard against paper need them to speak back
explain me tell me what I am doing here
not as a god but as a god might be—
rip out blind pages from their stapled spine
tear them into clouds of white confetti
pale stars on the patio
under the moon's unknowing eye
that sees through me

ARRIVAL

Zipping up a brown leather suitcase—no:
he was packing it with shorts, shirts, socks,
he was leaving—my father, standing above
the open suitcase on their bed, which is me
standing over a suitcase, which is any
man not knowing what to do next—I woke
& saw him coldly decide,
no, not decide but stand there, head bent, who
seemed always half in a dream, half somewhere
neither my mom nor I could reach—where would he go
if he could close it, lift it, carry it down
imaginary stairs in his sad head,
would he be dozing on an empty train
that speeds toward me and won't stop?

O, IT IS MY LOVE!

"*If* life is a handkerchief sandwich," then
A is to Z as B is to X, like Romeo's
"He jests at scars that never felt a wound."
"I, I, a scratch, a scratch" most people forget
or don't read and Juliet at a window
and that ridiculous But soft! What light
and all that other crap O speak again
bright angel—the truth about love is it kills
and I stand at the exit from what was
to what will be, but where is that? Why is
an old man saying this, shouldn't I just
accept acceptance? not one white blossom
on the idiotic pear tree I planted on the side of the house
no hope in the silence of the lost onlooker

BEING DEAD

In Jarrell's great poem Next Day
A middle aged woman suddenly sees herself—
I'm old she says that all I'm old.
As a boy puts groceries in her car
she sees him in the rear view mirror
not seeing her and sees the dead body
of her friend yesterday at the funeral...
the woman who still lives though the boy
does not see her sees herself dead
"granite among her flowers" and the boy walks
away and she is standing there talking to me...
it really isn't Jarrell who speaks but the woman
it's really not the woman among her flowers
but me reading being read by dead Jarrell

NO WAR

They say it's war but I know better it's how my father's eyes looked
    after a month in coma
I can't describe that faraway animal terror signifying no hope
    because a dog does not have hope
War my ass it's a Hollywood charade even the clip of two faceless
    soldiers without legs can't be real
Look at it you can see it's retouched the way a cosmetician would
    pump up a starlet's boobs in a cashmere sweater with falsies
See this wad of hundreds in my pocket my house my cars my
    beautiful dog copper downspouts Zen rock garden
I know better than to believe it's war when I stroll down a sunny
    street buy a friend a drink a shirt on sale at Saks
Also I flipped through an L. L. Bean catalogue last night picking out
    Christmas gifts—comforter fleece pullover slippers—
Where was war when I spotted a pair of hunting boots Gortex lined
    heavy cleated waterproof soles wool shirt
War? impossible I'm a man who likes to eat well travel take long
    showers read but of course my heart goes out in all its eloquence
    to all that suffering God I love finding just the right words
    religious words to make me feel virtuous words like "sanctity"
War fuck that there's no war it's abstract an invention it's not
    getting laid eating a steak slipping my plastic into a slot watching
    the bills glide out
In fact just today a friend sent me that dazzling photo of Rita
    Hayworth legs under her sitting on a bed in a negligee black lace
    top cupping the firmest fullest pointed most succulent breasts I
    ever saw white satin waist to her ankles forearms resting on her
    thighs
Her eyes look left at someone outside the shot an image behind her
    head cheap Technicolor hotel print of palm tree & cockatoo
There was no war when I tacked her up on my office wall today why
    don't they stop publishing fake front line snapshots interviews
    with bomber pilots they've screwed up TV with mendacious news
    reports interviews shots of bearded terrorists

I remember in 1943 my mother told me No war Stevie! seriously
    don't believe everything you read just have fun play with the
    cripple nextdoor do your homework stop masturbating so much
Tell me if there's really a war why am I going to dinner tonight at
    The Four Seasons why colossal shrimp why banks sending me low
    rate credit cards why do I dream of yachting Bahama cruises why
    do I still want to be richer and richer
Next time channel surfing I'll stop at the so-called war for a minute
    enjoy its real amazingly real images whatever grief or sorrow I
    feel war is necessary.

TO YOU

At night our bodies nearly touch in the big bed the goosedown
  comforter feels as light as the hand of God
I remember a smaller one in a different house where I slept alone in
  fear without others
I say light because God has no hands nothing except the world to
  define Him whatever we may say
Nights are always equally dark but the mind has degrees chocolate
  tar coal taffeta open grave thoughts that panic the unwary
But I don't care what it means as long as it continues or maybe I
  should say I believe the afterlife is right now since this moment
  need not be
Belief! what a word the only one that really applies to everything as
  Nietzsche knew and Freud who destroyed the word forever
Of course it all depends on who you listen to or refuse to listen to I'd
  like to be able to hear both at once
The way things are not being able to accept the way things are the
  way things are is God
Constantly on the threshold of revelation lamenting all raising
  hymns to all
Some days it's true even the coffee grinds are sacred nose hairs snot
  threads equal to the most exquisite blazing yellow leaf ruined
  soon where sweet birds sing
And in the midst of whatever might be deemed agonizing irremedi-
  able the world continues to give itself exactly as it is
For love of the earth is inescapable in surrender and *who we are*
  and *what is* are one no thought can contradict the peace of that
  perception

II

WINTER SHIVERING/MALLARME

This Saxon clock is slow and strikes thirteen among its
flowers and gods

Who owned it? Who dragged it here in ancient forgotten
coaches?

Unidentifiable shadows cling to the grungy windows

Who stared into the abysmal ice of your Venetian mirror on
the shore of tarnished snakes?

I know thousands of women have bathed the sin of their
beauty in this water

If I gazed into it long enough perhaps I'd see a naked ghost

Animal you often call me sadistic things

Spider webs clot and mingle high up in the massive skylights

Our cupboard's wretchedly old this fire scorches its
melancholy wood

Sun-bleached curtains weak chairs paint rubbed away frayed
embroidery

Pale engravings on the walls everything we own is old

Don't think about the spider webs evolving above you

"The grace of faded things" is my phrase for this

You hate new objects their garish audacity scares you you
would have to use them wear them down scar them
impossible for someone who hates action

Close the German almanac you read so avidly that lists every
dead king from a hundred years ago

I'll sprawl on the antique carpet my head cradled between
your charitable knees sister I'll talk to you forever

No more fields the streets uninhabited no world no people I'll
describe our furniture discuss it define the metaphysics of
chairs and tables for the first time

Milky webs shiver on the majestic skylights it could be the
moon I see tangled among the filaments

Or you or me

Or a new city barely conscious of itself blind

DEMON OF ANALOGY/MALLARME

Did you hear those unknown words singing on your own lips
cursed tatters of a ridiculous phrase?

I walked outside sensing a wing slip over the strings of some
fragile instrument linger then a voice "The Penultimate is
dead" descending note by note

Is dead   The Penultimate in that order the pause between
the two oblivion phrases fateful useless meaningless

Took a few steps heard in the void of sound the string
stretched taut forgotten instrument wing of glorious Memory
visited its feathers brushed my finger on the contrived
mystery

I smiled I used my intellectual hungers to beg for a new
subject of speculation

The phrase came back exact detached from an earlier fallen
feather or branch the voice changed into a voice that spoke
itself its own clear personality vibrating like a steel wire

I went with it reading it like the last words in a line of poetry

I made its speech my speech the silence after "Penultimate"
my anguished pleasure

Then the string snapped over the void ignorant of itself and I
contributed a sort of prayer—"Is dead"

Nothing could disrupt my favorite thoughts I calmed myself
by citing the dictionary—the last syllable (but one) of words
still unrenounced scraps of a linguistic task that makes my
noble gift weep when it's interrupted

Deceit sonority easy affirmation maimed me

I let desolate words ramble over my stricken lips I strolled
anywhere murmuring "The Penultimate is dead, quite dead,
the miserable Penultimate" to appease my grief

I saw my hand transparent mirrored in a shop window
gesturing as if about to caress...what?...my furtive hope
unfathomable magic

Now the voice itself was my voice the first voice ever heard
the only voice

Then pierced by the Supernatural slashed by its
indecipherable truth my soul transfixed shaken from its
throne

I looked up from the street in front of me a lute-maker's shop
vintage instruments hung on the walls arranged in the
window the pavement splashed with yellow fronds the wings
of feeble birds invisible in shadow

Like a madman I ran off condemned to wear black forever
because no one will ever explain The Penultimate

THE PIPE/MALLARME

I found my pipe yesterday meditating all evening on my work
lovely winter work

Cigarettes tossed away with childish summer joys into the
past leaves blue with sun and muslin my hard pipe between
my teeth again serious man dedicated to smoking a long long
time motionless born to concentrate on his work

Who knew that when I took the first puff on the neglected
thing I'd forget the big books I wanted to write

This friendly pipe hadn't been used since my return to France

I lived London inside myself last year gentle fogs that smell
like bittersweet ash seep through doors and windows stifle
the brain

My tobacco smelled like leather furniture sprinkled with coal
dust in a dark room where a skinny cat rolls around

Big fires the maid adding coal her arms warmed red clatter of
coals spilling out of the sheet-iron bucket into the iron scuttle
each morning

With the postman's solemn *knock knock* I came alive

Those sickly gray trees in the forsaken square outside my
window had no power to touch me

The sea crossed frequently that winter freezing on the bridge
of the steamer doused with spray black smoke

There I was my poor confused lover dressed in traveling
clothes beside me long dowdy dress the color of road dust
cloak drenched matted on her shoulders straw hat no feather

One stringy ribbon mangled by salt air the kind rich women
throw away the minute they step off the boat the kind poor
lovers retrim season after season

Around her neck she had rolled and knotted that repulsive
handkerchief we humans wave when they say good-bye
forever

MEMORY/MALLARME

No image of a family in my head black-clad orphan I roamed
near the unfolded tents of the quincunx fair

Did I feel this is how I should be did I feel the breath of the
future on my skin?

I forgot my schoolmates among the ragged hobo friends I
loved their dank smell made me delirious

Through the rip in the tent no choir singing no voice
declaiming love from a distance just the dramatic holy hour
before the footlights flair some brat wearing a hood like
Dante's too wobbly to perform with the others crawled inside
a loaf of bread sprinkled with soft cheese like snow or a lily or
another whiteness with wings inside it: impossible to put
words together—I would have begged him to let me share the
meal some famous old man picked at against a nearby tent
while he did handsprings back flips and other banal antics fit
for the day

He pirouetted in tights alert with nakedness and asked me:
"Your parents?—I don't have any.—If only you knew how
comical a father is...even when he wasn't eating last week the
ringmaster kicked his ass and he made his crazy faces..."

The rest of this poem is incomprehensible I can't write it—
something about how Papa bowls us over bites into the
chaste food of the very young No Mother? Alone? you don't
know anything—parents? hilarious idiots

I could hear the parade's trumpets cymbals drums reaching a
climax whoever "he" was he left I sighed suddenly
disappointed not to have parents

It was as if the pronoun "he" conquered reality a voice trying
to make sense of fragments of someone else's life a life I
thought was mine "he" and "I" were the same person in this
dream of memory memory of a dream

He was my real name opening onto a street of faceless
families high white far off peaks where the failures of
understanding resolve themselves into a silent palpable god
beyond god a new pronoun held up before

POOR PALE CHILD/MALLARME

Why do you yell so desperately that insolent shrill street song
drowned by cats lords of the roofs it can't penetrate the first
floor shutters or the rich silk rosy drapes hanging behind
them hidden from you

But you sing anyway continually tenacious self-confident like
a little man who works for himself alone depending on nobody
Do you have a father? you don't even have an old woman to
make you forget hunger by whipping you when you come
home without one penny in your hand

You stand in the streets dressed in washed-out grown-up
clothes too tall for your age much too thin for your age you
sing for food relentlessly you avert your malicious eyes from
the other children wrestling on the pavement

Your lament's so high-pitched your bare head rising with your
voice prays to fly off your narrow shoulders

Maybe it will one day little man after so much time yelling in
the towns you'll filch something crime's easy your pinched
fierce face have the courage to act out your wish

Nobody drops a penny in the basket your long hands dangle
hopelessly in front of you the world will make you evil you'll
steal kill

Your head still floats away still wants to fly off as if it knew
ominous fate and now your song strips us to the bone

You will lose it to the skies when you pay for me for those
worth less than me who quietly revel in your helplessness no
doubt that's your purpose in the world to starve steal kill we'll
see you in the papers

Oh we call you Poor Little Head with such pity because we
need you so we can be ourselves too sick with happiness to
drop the smallest coin into your sad basket

CHASM/BAUDELAIRE

Pascal's chasm splits me in two, I live it.
The world's an abyss—action, speech, reverie,
lust! Wind crashes through the enormous fear
of my hair crackling with electric fire.
Above, below, everywhere, ocean floor, shore,
silence panics space into ice;
God's wise forefinger won't stop scribbling
a nightmare in the dirt of my nights.
Sleep's dim cruddy pit swallows me—
flesh, mud, shit: I'm not sure what or where—
infinity feeds infinity outside my windows....
Each instant battered by dizziness,
jealous of numb nothingness, poor mind, pity me,
I'll never cleanse myself of Numbers and Creatures!

THE DRUNKEN BOAT/RIMBAUD

We sailed down the unexplored Amazon alone,
Indians nailed our guides to painted stakes
Naked, used them to practice archery,
Human targets riddled with feathered shafts.

How could I worry about my barbarous crew.
I hauled Flemish grain and English wood;
I left the bargemen and their gossip miles behind,
The river took my free mind anywhere.

The tides tore at my little boat and blew away
My cargo, I lived on land through winter,
Hull empty, those fragile floating villages
Along the shoreline were amazed by our joyful shouts.

Lighter than cork I danced on waves,
The storm baptized my sacred awakening;
Waves boiled endlessly on the sea bottom,
The lanterns' idiot eyes couldn't reach them.

Green shit spurted through my seams
Sweeter than sour apples to a boy;
It washed off stains of puke and cheap wine
And sucked overboard my anchor and wheel.

Since then I've plunged into The Poem
Of a milky sea clotted with stars,
Gorging on greenish blue where wreckage
And a brooding corpse often swims by,

Where slow ecstatic rhythms, dyed white,
Blaze in noon sun stronger than alcohol,
Vaster than the infinite music from above
That ripens the stinging wounds of love.

I know the sky slashed open by lighting, waterspouts,
Relentless surf, I know the night,
Know sunrise widening like a continent of doves;
I've seen what men merely imagined they saw.

I've seen the sun sink below the horizon, its terrifying
Mystic signs, and actors in a Greek tragedy
With muscular violet arms set on fire
The fluted shivering waters million of miles away.

Listener, I touched astounding Floridas
Mingling of human-skinned panthers' eyes with flowers,
Clutched rainbows stretched like infinite reins
Tugging at glaucous flocks on the ocean floor,

Seen whales rot in reeking marshes
Nets of reed flung over the pathetic corpse.
Waters brawling with each other in clear calm!
Yellow horizons swarming into indifferent voids!

I watched the deeps bellow and stampede the land,
Cattle with flames for tails, gigantic eyes,
But never believed Mary could walk on water
And close those foaming muzzles with her hand.

And glacial silver suns, red skies and seasick stars,
Nauseating wrecks collapsed in brown gulfs
Where giant snakes swarming with maggots
Drop black-perfumed from crippled trees.

If only I could show children those waves,
And gilded singing fish gliding in emerald;
Foam roses have blessed my pointless roaming,
Imperceptible winds have changed my arms into wings.

I was like a beggar on his knees. Then heaven
Dissected me the way my mother did
When I'd be sick in bed too nervous
To concoct my great visionary poetry.

And there were days when everything was nothing:
No islands, no gull droppings on my cannons;
No golden flower cups trying to seduce me.
I touched myself repeatedly to prove I existed.

I strode the purple mists, steaming and free,
Broke through the wall of bleeding sky
Sprinkled with lichens of the sun and blue-black phlegm—
All poets love that jam the way they love their sperm.

I've wept too much; sunrise twists my heart.
Every moon and sun is bitter, cruel.
Drunk on love's sour laziness,
O Let my keel burst let me return to the sea!

If I want European water, all I'll get
Is a black pond against a twilight sky.
The cows are gone. A sad child kneeling
Launches his paper boat frail as a butterfly.

Waves, I can't bear it any more, drenched in your weary distances:
No wings to cut across the cotton carriers' wakes,
Nor swoop against the flags of merchant ships,
Nor dive past prison boats grazing their guns.

Urizen 16[B]

III

OLD PHOTO

The man stretched out
in a one-piece black tank suit
on the beach in Atlantic City
grips his son's right foot and hand
in his hands, lifts
his head to look at him;
the boy, in a white suit,
sitting on his belly
smiles left toward the sea or anyone who
might be there—then, now, tomorrow—
P U S H O, a casino skill game
popular in 1937
(you underhand pitch a wooden ball up
an incline at different size numbered holes)
advertised in blurred gray letters high
on the boardwalk behind them,
their curly, thick, black hair
exactly the same—
who are we now,
one of us less than the fine sand,
the other seeing me and you?
I'd give my soul to be me again, there.

TIME'S LONELY

Think of the rainbow screen
which I love utterly and watch endlessly—
TV is like Baudelaire's life, really,
did that ever occur to you? like his syphed-up, rage-soaked nights.
I like to think of how he'd whap his cane
on promenaders' silk-hatted heads from behind
    or kiss his mistress's
lips—which ones?—or smoke hash or write
rhymed quatrains strict as despair's manacles,
hollow as your head in damp basement air.
Rats everywhere, *mon semblable,*
and someone's grandmother's bird's eye maple
    rocking chair, and fear,
bundles of fervid letters, IRS folders,
skis, rakes, cleaning solutions, plastic buckets, mops,
and yearning, pointless as the gold circles
rimming my mother's set of porcelain dishes
cushioned with newspaper in a taped cardboard box.
Down there again, I check the furnace's pilot light,
strike match after match,
rummaging through family documents—
my daughter's grade school themes—
and glimpse in a cube of sun
from a ground level window:
"I hate Emily Dickinson's poems, they're so weirdly rhymed,
    they hurt you..."
the rest of the sentence
torn off in the haste of packing probably
when we bought a shell in a poor neighborhood,
    gentrified it and moved in
which we were sure would protect us eternally
from poverty, greed, death, Baudelaire,
whose rhymes make time less lonely.
Wow—Tom Cruise piloting a Navy fighter!

Close-up of his black-gloved index finger
pressing the red button on the stick to waste an enemy plane
just like Baudelaire who did it with insanity,
boredom, art reviews, booze, his lethal mother—
confess it! *mon frère*—we want to be Christ-like sayings
    scrawled on a scroll
not channel-surfers fingering the remote.

STICKS

Despair was what I called
what drove me into my yard
to prove my love of nature, to clean up
winter debris—sticks mostly—
if I pushed my nose near leaves, if I bent down
astonished by detail: veins, cracks and lucent pools
trapped in the folds of rock, green stems, moss clumped on bricks,
first leaves the size of a baby's fingernail
popping out of every branch I came on—
maybe I'd live forever.
A Little Sally Raisin Creme Pie wrapper
had caught in the leaf tangle
of grapevines planted between us and our neighbor,
its dirty cellophane
note from no one to nobody nowhere.
That usually happens when I go out to commune.
I'll be hoping for the cosmic philosophical
and what I'll get is a fucking symbol—
a smiling teen piece in a miniskirt,
cunt whiffs of wet earth, moist
shiny bushes that have flourished overnight.
But I gathered leaves, stray
foam nuggets used to pad things in shipping,
plus, fallen dead from the trees, various sticks
that I clipped in half, and made into two neat piles
close to each other.
In the chilly late morning sun
their twin forms
glowed with Chinese mystery.
By that time I had worked up a hard-on
and held Little Sally's mouth on it for at least an hour
until, back inside, all I had to do
was lift her perfect body on to me.

THROUGH GLASS

Nothing below me moves except a fan blade,
starting and stopping on the roof, and one
fat pigeon wobbling across bright tar.
"can't stop hoping" "the next person you meet"
"face the harsh" "spiritual"
ooze their blank lubricious music,
each time a different meaning, different tone.
Bricks. Patches of weak sky.
Gunmetal clouds foam out from behind a cornice.
Queasy nothingness shapes caught in windows
flash, squirm.
Wonderful distant mirrors of no mind,
go fuck your absent answers.

RUBBER RATS

You know what it's like Sundays to
wash, brush your teeth, pull on pants and sneakers
then amble to the grocery store a few blocks a way
for juice, milk, bagels, newspaper, carry them back,
make coffee, toast—you know it. But the box of rats
brimming onto the counter as I left seemed
all wrong, vile, what's the word?
Black wild rats, fangs bared,
lunging in cartoon speed lines at babies,
blood spurting from puffy white thighs.
They gleam like a contained plague
seething in our sleep, which they did
in mine this week although I didn't actually see one.
Instead, a loving unidentifiable woman in a blue silk sheath,
stained near the neck, lifted it slowly over her head,
showed me her gorgeous naked rat-bitten body,
   motherly, not girlish,
and waited for me, on the verge of a smile, in this dream.
What deaths we create for others, what mirrors of denial.
Or what? How much of me is a rat free in the streets
urged on by the blessing of hunger or sick love,
who was the person who offered herself,
yes, no question, out of kindness,
and what else?

VINCENT

"Life is forever turning toward a man an infinitely vacant,
    discouraging, hopeless, blank side
on which nothing is written..." or
"...I always think that the best way to know God
is to love many things...one must love with a lofty
and serious intimate sympathy, with strength, with intelligence,
and one must always always try to know deeper, better and more.
That leads to God, that leads to unwavering faith..." or
"...I think that if one keeps one's serenity and good spirits,
the mood in which one acts is a great help." Of course.
    Oh yes. Yes.
Please, Vincent, say more. "You talk of the emptiness
    you feel everywhere..."
he wrote Theo—to help, to prove God exists,
to say to his brother: We must see Him, touch Him, believe
that His great wisdom made trees, bridges, fields, skies,
    ears, crows—or
"...a splash of black in a sunny landscape..."

"A caged bird in spring knows quite well that he might
    serve some end;
he feels well enough that there is something for him to do,
but he cannot do it..." "One cannot always tell what it is
that keeps us shut in, confines us, seems to bury us, but still
one feels certain barriers, certain gates, certain walls..."
    "Do you know what frees one from this captivity? It is very deep
    serious affection. Being friends, being brothers, love,
    that is what opens
the prison by supreme power, by some magic force. But without this
one remains in prison." Please, Vincent, say more
"What am I in the eyes of most people?...a disagreeable man, the
lowest of the low. Very well...then I should want to show
by my work what there is in the heart of such an eccentric man,

of such a nobody" "...a Robinson Crusoe or anchorite...otherwise
one has no root in oneself, and one must never let the fire of one's
soul go out, but keep it burning."
Oh yes, Yes. What color is the soul?
"...a splash of black in a sunny landscape..."?
"...the mysterious brightness of a pale star in the infinite."?

FAITH

She was sitting up in bed, propped on three pillows, watching the
 tube as usual when I walked in carrying the tray
of orange juice, medium scrambled eggs, buttered toast, coffee with
 a dash of milk.
"Do you believe in anything," she asked. "I wish I did," I heard
 myself say, unhesitatingly.
Since then I've wondered what answer would have been right,
 though she didn't seem hurt or disappointed:
"I don't know why, but I love cartoons. I could watch them all day!"
I'd always make sure her tray was neatly arranged,
 with a crisp napkin,
I'd add extra touches—newspaper, magazine, flower—
pull a chair to the bed, watch her eat, glad to see her eat.
Her hair was perfectly combed each morning, lipstick and rouge
 sparingly brushed on. "When I'm dead I won't have anything."
Never to think, no eyes to see with, mouth to taste,
 never to talk to a friend....
There's an ineradicable fear
carried like an unborn child, concealed within me;
if I could give it to the world, embrace it,
I'd have faith, I'd be able to save others, whatever that means—
I wish I believed what I need to believe.
You don't let others know you hate their dying.
We want each other simply to be here.
On her first day out of the hospital a month after the stomach
 cancer operation
we were driving down to her place at the shore
when she spotted a row of freshly planted saplings all along the
 divider—"So beautiful!"
After she'd finish, I'd unthinkingly remove the tray,
 wash her plates, cup and
utensils immediately,
I'd wash them just to wash them, hold them there under the hot gush.

SLICE

One of us held the paper and scanned the front page, one leaned
    against the wall in front of her bed under the TV, someone left for
    a minute to stroll the halls and peek into other rooms.
Irises flared from a white plastic pitcher, a sunny day drenched the
    room, she lay motionless, calm, the tube in her wrist delivering
    one clear drop regularly.
On that visit, too, she stayed the same as long as we were there, we
    didn't say much, witnessing, attending—what's it called to watch
    one's mother dying, she's not awake, doesn't need you?—
you believe you must help her to go through it; must catch her last
    words, if any are spoken, to have wisdom you can quote, use to
    fathom your life, anyone's life,
and of course you can't tell on what day, what hour the end will be,
    and finally you go home.
We hung around that morning, just in case, whatever that means,
    obviously enthralled by the force taking her that resists interpre-
    tation, awed by its visual purity,
(the next morning at seven on the dot a call would come from her
    doctor to say she was dead, could they use the body for research).
As we were leaving for the day I picked out a slice of freshly cut cold
    orange from the plate on the bedside table, leaned to her ear,
    asked if she wanted it, and, at her nod and lips parting,
    inserted the fruit,
which she bit, sucked swallowed, opening her eyes, then looked at
    me as if I were really there, as if she really knew me, and, when
    I withdrew the empty rind, proclaimed with a kind of child-like
    whispered joy—"Refreshing!"

SHOESHINE

I asked my ailing mother if she beat me,
if she ever screamed at me for doing wrong things
or wouldn't let me go out to play
because of her fears.
I was trying to know why I feel terror
from a skin bump, a shift in the weather,
a sick look in a passing stranger's eyes.
She said, "I polished your shoes every night
but I never punished you if you got them dirty the next day."
"No, that's not it, Jesus," I moaned,
"Did you ever...were you strict, harsh, cruel, you know..."
"Well, if you threw rocks at people I'd give you a verbal lashing—
look this isn't going anywhere, you won't get the answers here."
And we changed the subject.
Those shoes, taken and put back while I slept,
still glimmer in darkness,
their deep sheen vibrates with promise of first light.
What can little black, brown or white shoes, immaculate
no matter what they picked up during the day, mean now,
again and again resurrected
like mock replicas of what I don't know?

BANDAGE

My mother acted like a god, crazy, because grown-ups *are* crazy,
she sat there banging the piano non-stop while my father
    and his mistress
jibbered about their love, she kept playing wildly
through their words. I must have been somewhere,
    but this came to me
only as a story so I'm embellishing, filling out a mirage.
I try to see her, two strong hands flitting across the keys
    almost an hour,
my father and his girl side by side on card chairs,
explaining, their lips working in the stunned silence of my distance,
    then, now,
a Van Gogh sunflowers on one wall, a Cezanne Mont
    St. Victoire on another.
Where was I, why was I always out of sight
when murderous things happened? What was she playing?
    Popular? Classical?
Where was my little bull terrier? What was the weather?
    What meanings stung the air?
How did my mother's face look when I burst in finally
    out of nowhere?
Something is very wrong with this world of people.
Maybe you can tell me what it is, if you agree, maybe you
have had such queer pain all your life, squirming in you
    like a hot wire,
and can't find speech for it either and believe you never will, believe
a blinding innocence was forced upon you, as if they
    bandaged your eyes—
sent you out to play or buy milk to "spare" you while they did it—
so they could inject it, right there, inside you
beneath the elegant thick gold petals and bluewhite hills of the
    Dutch and Flemish.

MILK

The baby nextdoor is crying, less than a minute.
I'm out back on the patio smoking a cigar, relishing the pale
blue calligraphic swirls swim off, dissipate, when I breathe out.
I drink a second glass of red wine, clutch one of the grapevine's
    limbs twisted into the trellis behind my head
its floppy leaves wider than a baby's hands.
The silence of no crying wakes me now
may sound strange, but to me it means an anecdote my
    mother told me:
when I was that age. Her neighbors, mothers too, would phone her—
"Hilda, why don't you pick Steve up, he's been crying for hours?"
She explained she let me cry like that to teach me
"I couldn't have what I wanted whenever I wanted it."
We were sitting in her beachfront condo, eating shrimp,
discussing "...your father's constant vicious adulteries..."
when she volunteered this fact about feeding me.
Since then suicide's dream of white consciousness
like a calm hand steadies my mind
poised between here-now and insanity.
Twilight glows pink above housetops; the leaves breathe cool.
I've finished my cigar and wine. Flicked the butt into the bushes.
Their essences on my tongue—how can I say it?...are
the yard ecstatic greens, the silence good,
the idea that someone is comforted...

THEY LIVE IN THE LEAVES

Who are they? Birds? Us? Flutterings
among the bright and shady greens?

I can't say what I know, what me
is out there in those flutterings,

what sense of things beyond this "self"
never wholly itself

that wants and wants and wants and is
the want it wants.

DEATH

After my father died my mother gave me his watch

Round 18 carat gold case white face sweep-second hand a
    black needle

Her gift on his 60th birthday

It surprised me she did it considering their strife my love for him

On the day we moved into our new house I gave it to my wife
    spontaneous fleeting love did it

Beautiful on her wrist

Now gone from her wrist

My father's non-existent wrist

Cannot be circled by the watch again unless air can wear a watch

Who is wearing his watch her watch this minute and where and why?

I see it left behind on a blue and white striped beach towel in Capri
    while one more Pagan vacationer plunges into the surf

Or caught in a tangle of broken watches in a box in a showcase in a
    Camden jewelry store

Or I can dream it back onto his wrist coarse dark brown arm
    hairs blue veins rivering the tops of his hands

Or it might have been used for parts black alligator strap winding
    stem bezel crystal

Not that my father would care who surely did not think watches
  could inspire belief in a deity while each hour flees

Right now someone is lifting turning up his left wrist to see what
  time it is

On the way to seeing a woman he loves or a business lunch

The bracelet of pale skin the band leaves when he takes off a
  watch to shower forget the watch step out dry off dress

Nowhere now my father's wrist would like its watch back please

Nothing comes back not even an idiotic watch that tells you when
  to be where what time it is where you are

Helplessness quells the I to its opposite blue incessant
  interval streaming away

YOU COULD SAY

...you could say that you did not ask to be here and revenge yourself
you could say wire and hair beat each other in to a raining hell you could
say "testicle" every five minutes to yourself in the middle of a
conversation on the street in a restaurant while taking a shit anywhere
until you became the hairy thing itself shrinking up inside
you after you come God what beautiful balls you have she said and I
thought my hard-on would give me a stroke testicle testicle testicle
that should take your mind off the fact that soon you will not be here
does it? evaporate self-consciousness the terror of no self-
consciousness "love every loss" says Ammons and I can if I'm allowed
to sing testicle testicle whisper it into a stranger's ear she's standing
next to me at the ATM and she is actually grateful "Thank you sir it
sounds like the churchbell in my town in Iowa Sundays even my
mother would say to me 'Mary doesn't that sound exactly like
testicle?' and we'd laugh and watch my father roll his eyes cover his
balls with the hand inside his pocket I wondered if the priest in his
black gown wore underpants if not he could fondle his naked testicles
through the slit in his robe while spitting out a sermon in confession
very religious I'd say reverent holy divine" yes the testicle is a singular
phenomenon scrotum too is a fine word to take your mind off death
blot it out but at the other end of the scale testicle more soprano
scrotum closer to bass it might be best to utter one after the other at
five minute intervals in as many different tones and speeds as possible
to make their music infinite one first then the other then reverse
the order O say can you see by the dawn's early testicle by the
twilight's last scrotum that's what will happen that pair will creep into
famous texts delivered to large groups increase very very slowly over
the years until in every head almost unnoticed those two words will be
the only ones left The lord is my testicle He leadeth me beside the still
testicle He prepareth a scrotum before me yea though I walk through
the testicle of testicle I shall feel no scrotum and I shall dwell in the
house of the testicle forever

TO MY SON

In the car, bitterly yearning for a kind woman
I hadn't seen in years, I turned to the driver—
"I'm leaving, I'm leaving. Let me out, now!"
But first, I asked where my son was,
and he jumped up from the floor, perched on top of my fist,
a white mouse I bent my lips to and kissed
and held against my cheek.
The car sped on. There was a feeling in this dream,
just before he appeared, of grief, and I
can't recall—something, something.
My wife was at the wheel. We battled. Rain.
Trees, blacktop, hillside seen through a blurred windshield.
A line I wrote in my sleep is lost too,
its cold plain words, like these, worthless terms of meaning.
What happened before the scene in the rain-drenched car
is me straddling a woman in bed, biting
very very gently through sheer white silk
her nipples, then cut to the road, wife, mouse,
anguish. Whose voice or face keeps signaling,
crying out from a great distance in the mind,
from a life I know I should live? The sweet
poor beast that came when I needed my son . . .

NIRVANA

When I remembered each blessed word
Of the Brihadaranyaka Upanishad—
"...*not this not that* is the soul believe me
incomprehensible honey this thunder
is honey for all beings the Self is all..."
after I could recite this wild Sanskrit
text so flawlessly that whenever I took a shit
I'd think *this* stuff is Self too
fetid but still The Indivisible
making a beggar move his lousy feet
to let me by with my infected toe
Johnny Walker Black her crotch on my face
in all such ways didn't I tread the infinite
isn't that seething field of starlight me?

WINGS

In the modest plot I see them
kneeling to pick tomatoes, yanking weeds,
squatting between rows of broccoli, squash, beans,
Bill's pulled-back pony tail, Cathy's fine ass,
two sheds Bill built, rakes bunched against a wall—
the Jew I am had to buy a Badminton set
for the clear space of grass next to their garden
where net, poles, stakes, chalk lines would be,
then shuttlecocks, no plastic, real feathers only,
at least six rackets—every summer
out there eating and drinking we would play hard,
& I, the oldest, I must say, beat the living shit
out of everyone—adults, teenagers, kids—
a great pro blessed with wings—in my head

VISIT

I see the mirror where I saw your face
made-up to die; you were shockingly thin
"like Auschwitz", you said, your rouge too red,
both lips like blazing rose petals; you stood
studying yourself, amazed that the face
was your face—but because it wasn't real
I thought it might be immortal, free of pain,
immune to the real you's disappearance.
I stood behind you in the clean blue room
watching you linger, brush your hair, touch up
your eyebrows, thinking, I think, that if you
stayed there you could never die—the bed
was tilted up, the bright steel wall sockets over it
empty, your brown paper slippers empty

UNTITLED

And in those brilliant notebooks by Camus
"the fear of suffering" and the woe of love
"destroy oneself in suffering because you dared
to destroy others." and several quotes from Weil
such as "one doesn't enter truth
without having passed through one's own annihilation,
without having lived at length in a state
of total and extreme humiliation."
line 9 should say *No, No?* its nada tune
line 10 exterminate the thirst for love
11 kiss your wet transcendent lips
12 mollify redeem covet the dead
not one word exists that can say what is
not a single word can say it

FIXING IT

A beetle nibbling at a leaf is out
to finish all the green that's there now soon
one falls on it then two or three attack
start at the edges and enlarge the hole
until its exquisite symmetry is gone
jagged and formless its impending death
makes it look worthless—those I destroy
unconsciously nearly every time I spot one
on a low branch or bush my thumb
and index finger pinch the stem bottom
strip it off so the world's the way
it was before it learned it's here to be eaten
lick the juice off both stained fingers
nothing but perfect leaves left to be eaten

VARIATIONS ON CLARE

I am...rain saturates the streets and trees
I am but...avid to live obsessed defeated
I am but what...I find Thy whole hand light
I am but what I...heard unheeded am
"For entire days I have the most frightful
opinion of myself." I am "We hope
to live but never live" Camus Pascal
sometimes I feel they're one man
"I am but what I am none cares." Streets trees
a finch's eye blinks in my good binoculars
mutter of drainpipe none cares or knows
"alone and more alone on Christ"
I call cried Hopkins, is but what I am
none cares none knows none cares or knows

READING A LINE

"Making my minde to smell my fatall day";
Christ who could have written that how could he
have heard the notes that made it possible
the poem's about flowers how George Herbert
identified completely with a bunch
of "posies" in his hand then as they withered
penned "deaths sad taste" "farewell deare flowers"
he sang to them we do not have that power
that sincere tenderness instead we hate
others ourselves—Donne's love-stricken line
"So if I dream I have you, I have you"
echoes, lingers I don't know why—
I'm trying to say I don't know how we bear
our absolute eternal not being here

ON THE BEACH

Could it be that the purple words I saw
on the thin white fluttering banner
trailing behind a biplane over Longport NJ
actually said GOD EXISTS YOU ASSHOLES
SUNNING YOUR TITS AND TORSOS ON THE BEACH
YOU ARE INHABITING MY PROPERTY
No one stirred believed they read what they read
the sea was wild that day raw shark gray
the clouds three-dimensionally sharp-etched miraculous blue
surrealist clouds in a twenties cartoon
teeny toy boats frozen on the horizon
not one baked head on fire with the need for God
let alone the idea of an all-knowing Greater Being
just hats umbrellas legs glossy with sun tan lotion

MY GRAVE

Certainly not in a graveyard among strangers
though after death we're all the same,
certainly not with a headstone or marker
my father wanted his ashes thrown
from an airplane over his mother's grave.
Since I will not be anywhere
why should where my ashes are matter?
Except what if someday I'll want to find me
and chat and gossip and argue about poetry
what restaurant to go to—I could even
say to myself Christ you look great for your age
young girls would still want to boff you
so keep what's left of me in an urn...
No let the wind take me everywhere to everyone

INTERPRETING A LINE

"Love bears it out until the edge of doom"
I want to breathe that line I want to be
the flesh and guts the mind that hammered it out
bequeath it as a kiss to everyone
through the tiniest act—washing a soup-caked spoon
slicing tomatoes finding the right words
for the waitress who wishes she were somewhere else
the way she knows she damn well better smile
a certain way to make me leave a tip—
whatever kind of love it is isn't it good?
I folded clean towels last night and stacked them tidy
I sprayed the sink until not one speck of food was left
I have nobody to bear it out until the edge of doom
don't know if I alone am hard enough

AFTER

What we become buzzed in me, insatiable fly
of fact, of truth, seeking some crumb in me
that could be my father's face, that hummed Soon
when I die nothing of him will be here,
his face I see right now inside my head
less and less here, then I thought of my daughters
who still have in them the ice cream parlor
he took them to Saturday afternoons, and they,
too, my aging children, will be gone—
I was on the street and stopped, stood there, stayed
there, as if to say Why walk? Which way?
and looked him in the face, stared though his face,
stared into space through traffic, buildings, air,
asking myself where he would be after me.

FROM ALEXANDER BLOK

"How painful it is to walk among men,
pretend to go on existing" buy razor blades
shave shower pull on socks underwear Levis
pick out a shirt take pills open the book
Purity of Heart Is to Will One Thing
search it for a millionth time "is patience not
precisely that courage which voluntarily accepts
unavoidable suffering?" absorb it
don't merely mouth the world's like an idiot
slip on old loafers scuffle to the door
collect yesterday's mail rummage the fridge
for what I really want to eat but what?
an old brown grape yoghurt a gulp of Pepsi?
close it my face hazy in stainless steel

HAND

I hold out my open hand waiting for it
to fill with flowers or another hand
to hold it in a violent waterfall
to be given money or a soft kiss
but nothing comes nothings fills up my hand
I slip it back into my empty pocket
I reach out to touch an innocent dandelion
among others growing beside the road
but my hand is still just my hand common
and lonely it has nothing else to do
nothing that matters anyway turning on
a faucet brushing crumbs off a table
smoothing my hair my hand remains a hand
holding nothing a hand doing nothing

CLEAN-UP

Where the pushers lived is a field now,
an entire square block leveled, neighbors fencing off
sections of ground for flower and vegetable gardens,
constructing a kind of ramshackle Eden.
Some citizens have set bricks into the ground to mark off their plots
or tied chicken wire to sticks, from broken broom handles hung
    string, fluttering cloth strips,
a few have even put up hand-painted signs announcing what they
    intend to grow,
here and there fresh dark topsoil has been dumped into pyramids,
go close you'll smell the bitter depth of beginnings that stings
about two blocks north of my house across from the pediatric
    neurosurgeon,
a block west of the arrogant pro-active lawyer's red Honda
plastered with do-this do-that bumper stickers,
where daily the furious toothless woman in bedroom slippers
silently walks past her son sprawled drunk on a steam grate.

ON THE COURT

Don't you know we're all going to become Zen Masters
who know how to meditate themselves into heaven
still attached to the body tingling singing winging
away into nowhere where the "I" is pure peace
and the "I" is my green birch tousled by the wind
is the sound when you enter that placeless place
think of it as a racket ball court all
the walls white you the racket the ball white light
ready to play but you keep waiting alone
the guy who was supposed to show up for the game
half-bombed at some crummy bar so you
play yourself as if he is there that's meditation
and Samadhi as you smash the hard black ball low into a corner
whether or not you are quick enough to reach it

MYTH

Behind everything—windows, doors, walls—like a dim face,
the myth of a better life exists, but it seems like death
beckoning, trying to wreck what you've worked years to build.
You feel it will kill you when, in fact,
it may be the life you were meant to live and haven't.
All these years living the wrong life. Is it possible?
You've been good—your ass pinned to the chair to write:
poems, letters, checks to pay bills—
so good yet so instinctively punished by hands you finally see are
    yours, miraculous old fingers
with their three bitten nails, long blunt piano fingers.
Now you're sixty. Now you are driven to decide.
Now you've been resurrected by the absolute silence of God.
Now you can't flee time's lesson—that the end
is here now while each puny syllable appears
like notes heard by a blind man, sung by a beggar in the street.
It's like stepping into a dark room before the eyes adjust—
things almost exist, space almost exists, you almost exist.
But a fresh inkling of love, a star
cuts its pure objective passion across the sky of your heart,
and on this conscious Tuesday you wonder what to do with the time
    that's left,
how to give up the self you know.
This one moment sitting in a chair, standing, walking, never ends,
has always tried to make you see that, hear that,
in the trivial daily decencies and secrets of your life.
This bit of time outweighs the clock,
this instant equals the great sigh of freedom
that lately calms you as if you possessed a different body.
No one knows what to do, and we all do it endlessly—
O salvation of not having died quite yet in each transit of breath.
Because we can't find terms for this maybe we will never
really live, but we get glimpses, hear it
in the simple abrupt hymn of leaves or a child's cry in the distance,

and the star that wakes my heart again
is a shield of beauty and I step forth without fear into the streaming
    flesh of time
and place my mouth tenderly against its mouth, that will devour us.
This is not one of those Japanese outbursts on the edge of death,
of clear identity, that dissolves death, in which a few images rede-
    fine the human,
it's too Western to be sane or wise or useful.
I'm alone. May the peace and stupidity of having no ideas
unveil what I know but cannot see or name.
Impossible—to be, where every face, gesture, phrase, shines
in a unique necessity of its own, which you cannot condemn.
Whoever sustained his arrogant certainties without fail
across your naked back with the sting of a whip
is dead. Now what? Who will you blame now? Fix your eyes on the
    wild sky,
which never thinks and is never the same, and ask it.

HYMN

We are moving closer to the speed of light but we do our jobs
    optician florist fruit vendor bum
the world is cut in half and we don't know it black on one side white
    on the other new love arriving in microscopic doses
not through our skin not through ingesting chemicals
spirit has ignited the human world which equals the square root of
    82 the need to kneel in a pool of mud
still responsible seated at our desks making a living serving popula-
    tions of the earth
we still eat breakfast shower put on clean underwear tie our shoes
    check to see how our hair looks read the financial pages headlines
    drink one last mouthful of orange juice before we step into the
    street
sometimes we copy the palms of our hands on the office copying
    machine while nobody's looking
sometimes we gaze out the window search other windows for
    cohorts but the glass is blind with sunlight
we are voyaging toward the one answer enshrined in our hearts
    for thousands of years the unheard urgent words the end of our
    waiting
doctrine of immortality creed of the meaning of pain principle
    of the organization of matter theory of nature's intrinsic gift of
    unconsciousness
until the mystery of being no longer haunts us
lean on no scripture for an understanding of this it is
    happening to you now
forget immaturity forget freedom forget familial wounds
without preludes of explication without verbal pointers even the
    phobia of self-knowledge tamed by this boundless power to fuel
    our phase in the history of existence
like pictographs on bone like the cute face of a squirrel like a finch's
    innocent habits of quickness
we are close to the speed of light not feeling the least inversion of
    self flicker of fear

prayer may be the cause & its enemy the arrogance of self-sufficient
    greed one man saving 80K of pennies in beer barrels another
    worth billions the hundred-year–old woman who saved every
    newspaper she ever bought since the age of 16 tied in bundles
    stacked to the ceiling until they hid the walls
citizens like those readying the cosmos for transubstantiation
    to instill the secret of time's actions and time's opposite in the
    human heart wrecked by despair
I say unto you was uttered by someone by something beyond us
    and *The Lord is my shepherd* but
you and the light will enact the presence of Messiah bring The
    Presence before us in a fusion of impossible theories needs
all things will look exactly the same nothing will change the way we
    live yet we will know how to bear it for the first time not
    Nietzschean redemption of affirm all re-live all as it was not
    Christian salvation not this or that system
liken it to those baffling instances of inner peace that simply happen
    to the way seasons change to the activity of clouds
describe any table words are eyes hear any person's voice eat drink
    walk sleep buy an expensive hat
the word eternal at last a fact among facts whatever form it takes
    trivial as eyelashes or dirt
think of the anguish of your hunger that has had one object—to
    place you in the
blameless hands of mercy.

IV

VARIATIONS ON A THEME BY WITTGENSTEIN
for Stanley

1.

"Save me, save me, I know you can save me!"
that most transparent expression of the void's

maw as one slides into its unimaginable infinity
like a fruit crate rushing down the ball-bearing rollers

of a loading chute as I upon your nakedness
am revealed invited by death even though

I hold your hands above your head
while the end says come inside me love and fear

the vulnerable sense of otherness the trouble with love
that identifies so completely it enters another's skin

is it's the grief of mortal consciousness aware
that it exists and soon will enter the universe

2.

Since the world is independent of my will whose will
forces me to cut this apple on a plate what will?

the last problem is surfaces and how to break through them
what heaven of metaphysics is stored inside or hell of nothingness

when my mother died Larry Beizer her doctor called
7 am "Steve, Hilda died. Can we use her for teaching?"

"Feeling the world as a limited whole—it is this that is mystical."
6.45 of the Tractatus whose last five pages like Bach's Partitas

seem to resolve everything not that the insomnia of daily
consciousness isn't still a cage of rats fixed to our heads

"Death is not an event in life: we do not live to experience death."
outstrips Christianity then why be terrified of it

just because we die and do not experience it unlike
everything else except surgery no one's life is an object

subjectivity of the western kind has us
trying to turn around and see ourselves as someone else

3.

To be here to have been here—and the world between
as I experience it I could reach out to touch my mother's face

and it would not be there having not reached out for it
for years it has not been anywhere

father I confess last night in a dream a 12 year old girl
fondled my prick and licked it until I came

a dull white liquid spurted out of the purplish head
the wish to disappear which is the true metaphysical wish

to start with LW gave his sister all his money his silence
in classes was a form of non-being he cleaned his floors

with wet tea leaves when *he* they grew less bright
the idea was to eviscerate phenomenon

as interns must have lifted out a first inch of intestine
then the other parts of my mother's insides

closest to that is a kiss or sexual penetration or homicide
why there is no narrative in Wittgenstein he explains

in the poignant humble preface to his Investigations
"I have written down all these thoughts as *remarks,*

short paragraphs, of which there is sometimes
a fairly long chain about the same subject, while I

sometimes make a sudden change jumping from one
topic to another.—It was my intention at first

to bring all this together in a book whose form
    I pictured differently
at different times. But the essential thing

was that the thoughts should proceed from one
    subject to another
in a natural order without breaks. After several

unsuccessful attempts to weld my results together
into such a whole I realized that I should never succeed...

my thoughts were soon crippled if I tried to force them on
in any single direction against their natural inclination....

The philosophical remarks in this book are, as it were,
sketches of landscapes....Thus this book is only an album....

It is not impossible that it should fall to the lot of this work,
in its poverty and in the darkness of this time,

to bring light into one brain or another—but, of course,
    it is not likely.
I should have liked to produce a good book. This has not

come about, but the time is past in which I could improve it."
no narrative except patching together inventing

a design of how you want to be seen be believed but
    the words
used are so tattered thin the weave so distorted

the emphasis on loss so central that to define a life
is a sacrilege of unintended blame brutality I

extol the supremacy of "the pure lyricism of shamebred music"
and do not try to break through by telling a story

4.

For those who now abide formlessly among
stars leaves ash lovers trying to forget

themselves for them who inhabit all I would become
them if that would be meaningful to them who do not think

or feel with me everywhere as nothing since when I'm snuffed out
now near the bottom of the candle what remains

of them in me will evaporate with me no matter how much love
I tried to train myself to feel attempting to become them

again and again while alive what matters is not that they lived
nothing will become of any of us who we were what we did

the fact that I have eaten made love written sung
    said to a friend
I love you don't worry it will all work out we are what is

before the music starts after it ends the silence that reaffirms
the world that watches us when we die with blind cold eyes

exactly like the stars we worshipped all our lives
because they did not care they simply burned

5.

"What we cannot speak about we must pass over in silence."
his famous final statement but I've always

thought of it differently—"What we speak about
we thought we could not but we did." like that clock two wooden
    pigs

one blue one pink fucking on the kitchen wall in Mighty Aphrodite
    the atmosphere
of innocence wafting off the tall hooker Woody beside her on the
    couch

"Would you like a blow job?" she warbles in her adolescent voice
his kooky hands trembling absolutely impossible all of it yet there it
    is
a cartoon metaphysics of the everyday something like that
happened to me one late afternoon sitting at a dark bar

with an executive interested in helping non-profit
    corporations
discussing poetry's need for money and out of deep left
    field I hear

in a discreet whisper "I want your cock in my mouth."
I can tell you—What we *can* speak about we must *not* pass
    over in silence

6.

Malice of galaxies of disease of the wrong parents of poverty
listen you cannot hear it the soul loosening

its grip on you just as I listened to my mother mangle Brahms
on her Steinway while I put my ear against the warm finned plastic
    radio

by my bed some voice in me always babbled like the
   young woman
dying of leukemia in the room next to my mother's

I drifted in "Why me?" in a weak whisper "It isn't fair."
   I answered back
and thought of Darwin many times Darwin's godlessness Oedipal
   abyss

the loud piano and my father where? I wore cotton
   flannel pajamas
and loved the glow of the dial yellow with the decal
   of a red bird on it

and let myself slip into the black wall across the room
which is that poor woman's pain still and always will be

"I have been here in the Moon-light,
I have been here in the Day,
I have been here in the Dark Night,
And the Stream was still roaring away."

means to me that wall across from me spilling into its depth
is where I am like one of the black keys

7.

The numbers on the lottery ticket in my wallet like
   faded code
would decipher me if I could decipher them

why I am me why I did what I did
why the noose of regret is tight around my neck

in pairs they cross the ticket double rows
like ugly singing floating out of a barber shop

you hand it over to the girl behind the machine
she punches it in 3 bucks you invest again in nothing

bullet in the brain a cold beer vodka someone who loves you
calls the bird in my yard singing like a cheap whistle Stevie

church row houses Laundromat Puerto Ricans'
    block-long garden
bus groaning up 20th three neon beer signs Bud Miller Coors

"Our life has no end in just the way
in which our visual field has no limits." (—6.4311)

8.

Because each of us craves the amorality of the infinite
we are not ourselves but obscure beings with nothing to lose

we see the = sign as a sacred link to
"God does not reveal himself *in* the world."

should be enough considering language's failure
to give us more than itself when used to produce

metaphysical propositions but we are left with the steamy
mirror of speech gum stuck on a shoe

and want to fuck the earth like moles some would call it nostalgia
the black wall securely rooted inside us

so we can't have or know that apparently distant thing
we'd kill to own like a beach house or a Lamborghini

"There are, indeed, things that cannot be put into words.
They *make themselves manifest.* They are what is mystical."

we wait for the manifestation although
those things already are manifest now why can't we see them?

temporal immortality of the human soul its eternal survival after
   death "I hate reality, but it's the only place you can get a good
   steak."

"For the world is Hell, and men are on the one hand
the tormented souls and on the other the devils in it."

"...nothing is more useful than to accustom yourself to
   regarding
this world as a place of atonement, a sort of penal colony."

how many quotes from geniuses does it take to heal me
let me enjoy the unremitting timeless doorless wall inside me

"These chairs they have no words to utter"
should be the motto carved above my door

some kind of yellow and black butterfly wavers over the
   red azaleas
sweet familyless negro housekeeper we loved who loved us

Ozalea forgive me for not having thought of you in years
I know how much you loved feeling part of our family

forgive me Ozalea your breast cancer our talks on the phone
you bedridden barely complained your lonely voice

your son dying in the house nextdoor of cancer too
I hear you silent agonized speak to each other through
   the walls

9.

"We should love the actualities, for we won't always
    be as we are."
crooned Vallejo whose "Pain grows in the world..."
    was never truer

"The solution to the riddle of life in space and time
lies *outside* space and time." should the stars speak,
    the galaxies?

Where did Wordsworth get "These chairs they have
    no words to utter"
"And I am alone,/Happy and alone" then "I do not wish
    to lie/Dead,

dead,/Dead without any company" where did the
    words come from
and all the lovers who could not possess each other

in a hell that will not let the other die faces we
    cannot disfigure
inside us possess us untouchable the intolerable loneliness

caused by remembered eyes lips hair that makes God an irresistible
    idea
"I believe more and more that God must not be judged

on this earth. It is one of His sketches that has turned
    out badly."
wrote Vincent to his brother but other forms of
    prayer or love exist

passionate insatiable crazed with irrational lust for example
"...no pursuit at Cambridge was followed with nearly so much
    eagerness

or gave me so much pleasure as collecting beetles.
It was the mere passion for collecting, for I did not
    dissect them

and rarely compared their external characters with published
    descriptions, but got them
named anyhow. I will give a proof of my zeal:

one day, on tearing off some old bark, I saw two rare beetles
and seized one in each hand; then I saw a third and new kind,

which I could not bear to lose, so that I popped the one
which I held in my right hand into my mouth.

Alas it ejected some intensely acrid fluid, which burnt
    my tongue
so that I was forced to spit the beetle out, which was lost,

as well as the third one." can you pray to
those words from Darwin's Autobiography they function

as a parable that represents the cause of each personal hell
and "God" the cure imbedded in that brief story

10.

Since the theme is death let me quote from LW again a euphoric
sentence that thrills me: "If we take eternity to mean not infinite

temporal duration but timelessness, then eternal life
    belongs to
those who live in the present." or as my mother blurted out

waiting for the hospital elevator "When I'm dead I won't have
anything." as if her possessions were possessed as if love ever works

Kafka's "...sex keeps gnawing at me, hounds me day
    and night..."
exemplifies the inevitability of secular crucifixion

who thought his writing was cruel though it was kind
the objects in my room make it possible for me to be here

I am alone I yearn for us to speak to each other but
"These chairs they have no words to utter"

POETRY AND PROSE POETRY BY STEPHEN BERG

Bearing Weapons
The Queen's Triangle
The Daughters
Nothing in the Word: Versions of Aztec Songs
Clouded Sky by Miklós Radnóti (with Steven Polgar and S.J. Marks,
    published by Sheep Meadow)
Grief: Poems & Versions of Poems
Oedipus the King (with Diskin Clay)
With Akhmatova at the Black Gates
In It
Sea Ice: Versions of Eskimo Songs
Crow with No Mouth: Ikkyū
Sleeping Woman (public art project with the painter Tom Chimes)
New & Selected Poems
Oblivion
The Streel Cricket: Versions 1958-1997
Shaving
Porno Diva Numero Uno
Halo (published by Sheep Meadow)
Footnotes to an Unfinished Poem
X=
The Elegy on Hats (published by Sheep Meadow)
Rimbaud: Versions & Inventions (published by Sheep Meadow)
Cuckoo's Blood
The Poetry Does Not Matter

ANTHOLOGIES

Naked Poetry (with Robert Mezey)
Between People (with S.J. Marks and J. Michael Pilz)
About Women (with S.J. Marks)
In Praise of What Persists
Singular Voices
The Body Electric (with David Bonnano and Arthur Vogelsang)
My Business Is Circumference: On Influence and Mastery